This Book belongs to :

-----------------------------

-----------------------------

# He said, She said

by daisy de villeneuve

**CHRONICLE BOOKS**
SAN FRANCISCO

First published in the United States in 2004
by Chronicle Books.

Copyright © 2001 Daisy de Villeneuve
and Pocko Editions

First published in the United Kingdom in 2001
by Pocko Editions Ltd.

Edited by Nicola Schwartz
Design by Olga Norman

Conceived, created, and designed by
Daisy de Villeneuve and Pocko Editions
P.O. Box 20190
London, England W10 5LA

Library of Congress Cataloging-in-Publication
Data available.

ISBN: 0-8118-4574-5

Manufactured in China

Cover design by Vanessa Dina

Distributed in Canada by Raincoast Books
9050 Shaughnessy Street
Vancouver, British Columbia V6P 6E5

10 9 8 7 6 5 4 3 2 1

Chronicle Books LLC
85 Second Street
San Francisco, California 94105

www.chroniclebooks.com

**For friends & family.**

I'd like to thank my family: Jan, Justin, and Poppy for believing in me, and particularly my grandparents for putting me through art school. A big thanks to everyone at Pocko. Plus Annette Olivieri, Michael Baigent, Peter Blake, Serge Beddington-Behrens, Susan Posen, Seth Redniss, Claire Sawford, Chris Kangis, and Ronnie Cooke Newhouse. Thanks to my Godfather, Stewart Grimshaw, who has been searching the world for the perfect man for me... (where is he?).

' you are responsible for who you choose to go out with'
he said.

'yeah, i know '                          she said .

' i've been told that anyone that dAtes him
is an idiot '                    he said.

'each  night we slept in the same bed and nothing
happemed '  she said.

'don't hold my hand' she said.
'are you trying t o keep me at a distance?' he said.

t you don't know me' she said.'I want to get to know you' he said.

'was she nice to yo u?'     he said
'she  was alright, i didn't have that much to say
to her , and she s   didn't have that  much to say
to me' she said

he lef t in the ~~middle-o~~    middle of the night.some

excuse about having to do his laundry and walk the dog

 in the morning ...........

'he dumped me, you wouldn't know what
it's like to be dumped'  she said
'what do you mean, i wouldn't know
what~~is~~ it's like, he was with me first,
any way ~~the~~ the whole thing is so weird'
i said.
'yeah, but HE  DUMPED ME' she said.

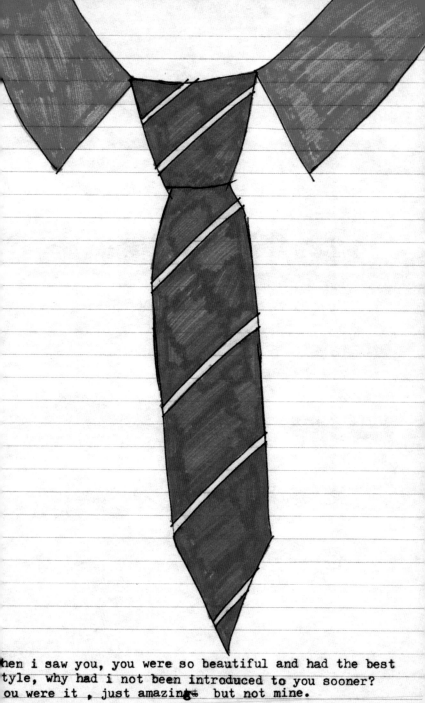

hen i saw you, you were so beautiful and had the best
tyle, why had i not been introduced to you sooner?
ou were it , just amazing  but not mine.

' since when have YOU had a boyfriend? '   he said.

he said that he wanted to do what he wanted to do.

when i last went to his house he invited that girl down

and his famie ly     just talked about how wonderful
she was, and i have never   beedn    back to their
house , it a    not like i don't have any feelings. i
felt like he was really condesending towards me, he was
so weird with me he acted like nothing had happened bet
us  and when i confronted him ~~on the subject he~~

he said i was passive aggeressive

i think about him all the time , and he calls me loads ,
we don't get too personal , but i really like him.

"he's a serial lover ." he said.

can we cut out the 'just friends' routine 'cos it's
getting really boring  and i really want to have
    sex with you.

he called back later , and left a
message on my machine saying,
 " too expensive, too little time and
 not under the right circumstances."

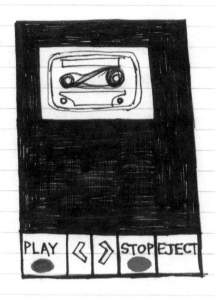

'he always slimes on my sister' she said.

'when you say you Don't Care, it really means that
    you Do Care'                    he said.

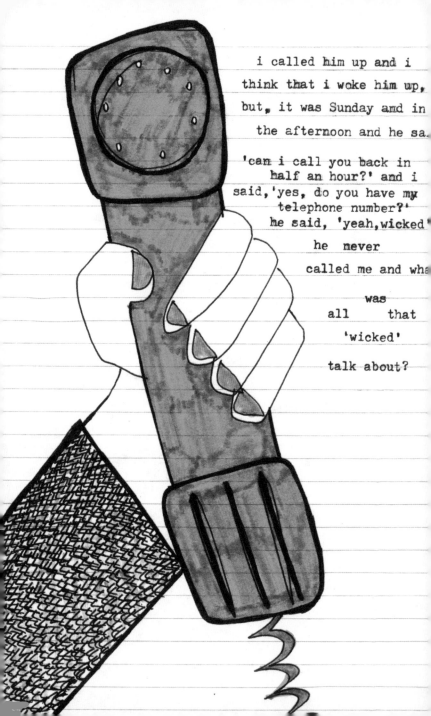

i called him up and i
think that i woke him up,
but, it was Sunday amd in
the afternoon and he sa.

'can i call you back in
    half an hour?' and i
said,'yes, do you have my
    telephone number?'
he said, 'yeah,wicked'

    he   never

    called me and wha

            was
    all      that

    'wicked'

    talk about?

'can i kiss you?'     she said
'it would be better if we didn't'     he said
'why not?' she said
     'it would be better     if we didn't'  he said.

'are you going to say , goodbye? to me?' she said
'why do we need to say a formal goodbye,
there doesn't need to be a conclusion' he said.

'boys  come and go, but friends, friemds are forever'
he said.

'i don't want to admit t hat   i have a girlfriend'
       he said
'why, are you embarrassed by me ?'      she said

' i think they thought i was    was    weird' he said
    ' maybe you are weird'  she said
   'well, i think you're weird' he said.

'i'm only going to L.A. it's not like
i'm never going to see you again.' he said.

721-8521

he walked into the party wearing aviators.
he reminded me of that   Carly Simon lyric,

    " you 're so vain"   .

" l   hate th e  word 'relationship'  ,    " he said

'how come i never meet any of your friends or family?'
she said. 'who said you wem would meet them?' he said.

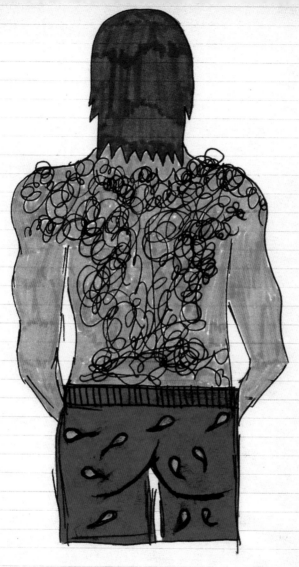

'yoyu didn't know i waas so hairy. did you?'
he said.

' i still  fancy you '            she     said

' i don't know what to say about that? '        he said

"Don't start Tripping on me now  GIRL."

           he said

'do you love him?' he said
'yeah, i think  so ' she said
'does he l ove you?' he  said
 'i don't know;  ?' she said.
  'do you love me?'        he said.

he said 'if i thought you were a freak i'd disappear,
         i'd run and hide.'

" I can't get him out of my Head." she said.

'you know he's going out with hw her',
are you upset?' he said.

' i'm not very good at having a girlfriend, or
        boyfriend.'    he said.

    'BOYFRIEND??' she said.
 'well, i haven't had a boyfriend before.'    he said.

'it's ju st not happening'    he    said.

'were you going to tell me?' she said

'i was considering it.' he said

i spent all my frequent flyer mileage going to
Pensacola, Florida and he didn't even kiss me

'then he said,i was the most flirtatous person he'd
ever met', she said.

'you should find a real man.
    i'm just a flake'          he said.

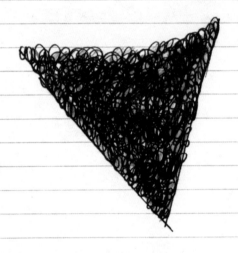

'you have a complicated vagina'     he said
'what do you mean?'      she said
'it's just complicated'  he said.

'you shouldn't believe everything you hear' she said
'i heard from the ~~seure~~   sourc e' he  said

'my thing with him just happens 'cos it's there.—Ply
Plus, I don't care. I am able to accept it for what
it is. actually, I hate it when he talks about other
girls' she said.

he's VERY       jet-set.

ho needs a boyf riend , when you can eat chocolate" he said.

'how come you didn't tell me about that?' she said

'why would i tell, e it'ss not something you would
go round telling people '                    i    said.

He rocks my world.

'you're being a typical girl'    he said

'you're so nice to me' she said
'i won't always be nice to you' he said.

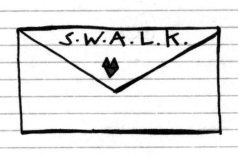

" But it's Valentines day" she said
"so, it's just another day." he said

'why don't y ou go out with him?' he said

'i don't want to go out with him.' she said
'don't let me hold you back' he said.

he said it was a , Deadend,

she said , 'you have to accept people for the way they are'.

i couldn't believe-~~hw~~ he was talking to me.
i got so shy that i couldn't speak.i had to
excuse myself and leave. i think i appeared
so uninterested      yet i was so interested.

'i told her to tell him, it was nothing serious' he sai
'nothing serioues ?.    she said. 'that's what i a

'you think that you're the only one' he said.

' I'm so obsessed ' she said.

she felt like he was always trying to impress her.

' i'm not a Saint '     he said.

'you are alwaysw    running away'    she said.

'WHAT exactly are you doing with HER .?. '    she said

'he only goes out with priviliged girls' he said
'i went out with him ' she said
'oh, i didn't know' he said.

" i usually know people for 24 hours "   he said

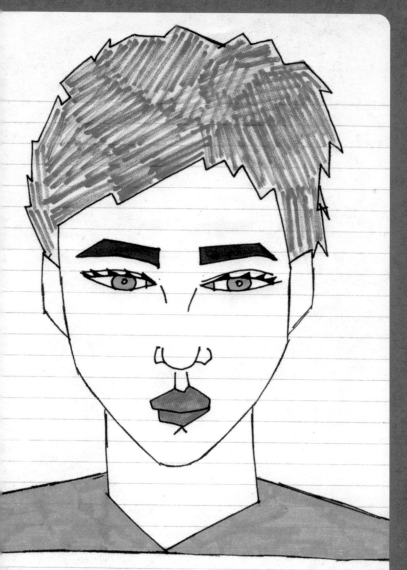

'once a month in the middle   of   the night i get a phone
call from him'   she said.

```
' i ss    should not have gone traveling.
  i should not have broken up with my girlfrien
              he    said.

' uh,      where do   i fit in ? '

              she    said.
```

h
he said, 'I only have sex with people that I really love.'
   'I was wondering does he love me ?' she
                                                  said.

He called me up amd

he    told me that he didn't want a girlfriend
right now, and that i shouldn't take it
personally etc etc.

     2     weeks later he went to Las Vegas
and got Married.

he said i was 'freaky' apparently  i shouldn't
interpret  this as an insul t.

he was alway s going on about, wamting to be
'BANNED'   from my house.

' i saw  him kissing a girl.'    he    said

'how do you know it was him?'      she said

'IT WAS HIM.  look, i'm only telling you so
 you can get over ▪  him.'        he    said

he rang out of the blue, he was the last

person i expected to hear from. he was
pretty  friendly considering the fact
 that he'd been a comple te jerk to me.

 if  i bring up ~~the~~  his bad behaviour
 he's all like 'lets be nice to each other'.

'apparently he came on to her'    he said.

'what's your name again'   he said.

she said that she's never had that problem before.

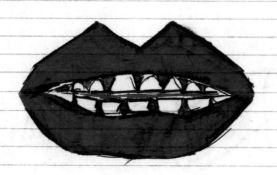

' don't use your  teeth '     he   said.

Justin de Villeneuve

**Daisy de Villeneuve** attended Parsons School
of Design in New York and earned a B.F.A. in 1999 from
the school's Paris campus. Her illustrations have appeared
everywhere from shoe boxes and fashion ads to her own line
of house wares. She exhibits internationally and is currently
working on a major solo show at the Fashion and Textile
Museum in London.